THE CELTIC WICCA SPELL BOOK

The Magick and Mythology of Celtic Witchcraft

By Didi Clarke

Disclaimer:
While I have performed all these spells myself, your results may vary.

CONTENTS

By Didi Clarke

*If you'd like to be notified when I publish a new book or have something exciting in the works, be sure to sign up for my mailing list. You'll receive a **FREE** color magick correspondence chart when you do! Follow this link to subscribe:*

https://mailchi.mp/01863952b9ff/didi-clarke-mailing-list

CHAPTER 1: THE PATH OF CELTIC WICCA

The fantastic and fanciful stories of Celtic gods and goddesses have been around for thousands of years. If you thought that the Greek pantheon was full of drama and intrigue, just wait until you meet the Celts!

And even though you might not realize it, these Celtic deities play a major role in the practice of modern-day Wicca. I would go as far as to say that Wicca and Celtic mythology are in some ways inseparable. And I'm excited to get to share these fascinating gods and goddesses with you.

In *The Celtic Wicca Spell Book*, we'll journey through the Celtic pantheon where you'll be introduced to gods like Dagda—the good god—and goddesses like Morrigan—the warrior goddess. However, this book is much more than just an explainer. It's a spell book too!

After introducing you to each god or goddess, you'll find an original invocation spell for calling down the power of that specific deity. These include rituals like:
- Invocation to honor the dead
- Invocation for bravery
- Invocation for starting a new chapter in your life
- And many more!

So Who Were the Celts? What is "Celtic"?

Before we get to the deities themselves, I think it's important to give a little background information about the Celtic people, Celtic mythology, and how they tie into witchcraft.

First, the basic answer—the Celts were an ancient group of people who lived in parts of Europe. These include areas like the Alps near France and Italy. But when most people think of the Celts, they're thinking about those who traditionally lived on the British Isles.

Now, the historical answer—academics typically consider the Celts to be any group of people that spoke a traditional Celtic language. This is useful definition because it accounts for Celts in unusual geographic locations (like those in Iberia).

For the purposes of this book, a majority (if not all) of the gods and goddesses I mention were traditionally worshipped in the British Isles.

As far as the term "Celtic" goes, it refers to anything associated with these traditional Celtic people—as well as modern-day Celts, like the Irish and Scottish.

How Do Celtic Deities Relate to Modern-Day Wicca?

Modern Wicca and the ancient Celtic religion are not one and the same. You'll find some misguided witches who believe that when they practice Wicca, they are practicing the same religion as the Celts.

However, this is simply not the case. And that largely has to do with the fact that much about ancient Celtic religion and its practices has been lost to time. How can we say we're practicing their religion when we know so little about how they themselves practiced it?

One thing that has survived into the modern day are their myths, their gods and goddesses. And this is were the link between Wiccan and the past begins.

Traditional Wicca and Celtic Wicca

These days, there are too many different branches of Wicca to effectively track them all! People have expanded upon this religion in some surprising and powerful ways.

However, one of the earliest traditional forms of Wicca was created by famed occultist Gerald Gardner. His form of witchcraft was not explicitly Celtic, but you can definitely see the influence that the Celtic pantheon had on his practice.

For example, we have the Triple Goddess and Horned God as the principal deities of traditional Wicca. While the idea of a triple goddess is not exclusive to the Celts, they definitely had their fair share of goddess who fill this role—and we'll see them in fuller detail later.

Additionally, Gardner sometimes referred to the Horned God as "Cernunnos" or "Kernunno"—names directly lifted from Celtic mythology. You'll find Cernunnos and his invocation in just a few chapters.

These and other things point to a Celtic influence within traditional Gardnerian Wicca. But the link between the two is made entirely explicit within the Celtic Wicca branch.

In Celtic Wicca, most practitioners leave the major tenets of traditional Wicca intact. It is instead an expansion of traditional Wicca by incorporating Celtic elements into the mix. This includes identifying the Triple Goddess and Horned God as the Celtic deities Brigid and Cernunnos, working with other Celtic deities, and a strong appreciation for nature.

Ultimately, Celtic Wicca is a blend of both old and new. It's not the traditional religious system of these ancient people, but rather is a reimagining of these ancient myths and deities. This sort of syncretic, eclectic approach is not everyone's cup of tea, but I think you'll find that this path offers a powerful mix of being connected to the past and excited for the future.

Discover Celtic Wicca for Yourself

Are you ready to experience the power of Celtic Wicca for yourself? These fascinating gods and goddesses await, so let's get started!

CHAPTER 2: BRIGID, THE TRIPLE GODDESS

B rigid is one of the most recognizable Goddesses of the Celtic pantheon. She was so popular, in fact, that when the Catholic church overthrew the traditional, Pagan religions of the region, the Goddess Brigid disappeared— but Saint Brigid took her place.

In traditional mythology, Brigid was married to the Irish king, Bres. Though they came from different tribes that hated one another, she believed that the love between Bres and herself could unite the warring factions. While this eventually came to be, much hatred and bloodshed came before the peace.

After the death of her son, Ruandan, on the battlefield, Brigid's grief was enormous. Her mourning was so powerful that it caused both sides to put down their weapons and forge a peaceful existence with one another.

In other legends, Brigid was said to have healed lepers, and there are a number of magickal springs in Ireland that bear her name and are said to have mystical, healing properties.

Brigid is the Goddess you want to turn to when you feel caught in the middle of strife that you can't control. She brings peace to those who are mourning and healing to those in need.

Brigid and the Triple Goddess

Brigid is referred to as a "triple deity." The idea of a goddess with three different aspects can be found in many religions, but it's particularly important within Wicca—the Triple Goddess is our primary and most essential female deity.

Within Celtic Wicca, Brigid typically fills this position.

Brigid Correspondences

Imbolg, one of the major Wiccan holidays, is dedicated specifically to her. You'll sometimes see it referred to as Brigid's Day instead.

She is worshiped as a Goddess of the sun, marriage, children, creativity, and, most importantly, prophets and seers.

If it's not already obvious, one of Brigid's most significant association is fire. Candle magick is a must when working with this fiery Goddess.

Plants that correspond to Brigid include blackberries, willow trees, rowan trees, rosemary, and grains. The natural world plays an important role in the Celtic pantheon, so approaching Brigid with a plant-based offering is a good idea.

Finally, Brigid is associated with the animals like boars, sheep, wolves, and swans—all creatures important to the daily lives of her earliest worshippers.

Brigid Flame Invocation

Centuries ago in Ireland, a shrine was kept for Brigid. In this shrine was a sacred flame that was never allowed to be extinguished. Nineteen virgin priestesses kept watch over the flame, and men were not allowed on the premises. When Catholicism took over the country, Goddess worship was banned, but the flame persisted.

In this ritual, you'll be recreating some of the power of this ancient sacred flame.

Items Needed
- 4 white candles
- 1 large red candle
- 1 bowl of water
- 1 white ribbon (large enough to tie around the red candle)
- Matches or a lighter

Begin this invocation by placing a white candle at each of the four cardinal directions in this order: east, west, south, north.

As you light each candle, repeat the following:

Holy flames surround this holy place. Brigid is near.

Next, return to the center of your circle and lay out your other items before you. You will need to consecrate your items before using them. First, bless the water by saying:

I bless this water with the power of the Spirit world. May it cleanse everything it touches.

Next, dip your fingers in the bowl of water and sprinkle some on the red candle. As you do this, say the following:

This item is pure and ready to work my will. I seal within it the blessings of the Spirit world.

Repeat this process with the ribbon as well as your matches or lighter.

Next, tie the ribbon around the middle of the red candle. If you know how to create a square knot, use that—this particular knot is effective for sealing in psychic power. Otherwise, tie it into a bow or other simple knot.

Now, light your candle and recite this invocation to Brigid:

Mighty Brigid, the light of your holy flame brings warmth to my soul. May its cleansing power raze the obstacles that obscure my view of the Spirit world. May this flame act as my bridge into the realm of secret wisdom. Show me the sights that I am meant to see. So mote it be.

At this point you should begin gazing into the candle's flame. Allow its hypnotic flicker to transport you to the realm of Spirit wisdom. Let your thoughts begin to wander where they may. As you move deeper into a meditative state, you may begin to see flashes or glimpses of a prophetic vision. Don't try to force anything—let these visions come to you as they will.

Prophecy is rarely straightforward, so expect what you see to be highly symbolic and cryptic. It can be helpful to have a notebook nearby to write down what you saw after the ritual is over.

When you're ready, begin to draw your consciousness back into the physical world. Slowly avert your gaze from the candle and allow your body to return to normal.

Extinguish the red candle and offer this thanksgiving to Brigid:

Go in peace, wise Brigid, for your flame has shown me much. I honor you for what you have allowed me to see. Blessed be.

Now, extinguish the white candles and close your sacred circle. Be sure to dispose of your water outside. If possible, try to practice flame gazing with the candle a little every day until it has been completely used. You'll find that the more you practice, the more your prophetic visions will improve.

CHAPTER 3: CERNUNNOS, THE HORNED GOD

Cernunnos is an ancient Celtic deity that has major importance in modern-day Wicca—we know him as the Horned God.

Along with Brigid, the Triple Goddess, Cernunnos makes up the second half of our dualistic conception of divinity. So needless to say, he plays a big role in many aspects of Wicca!

The Many Faces of Cernunnos

Like the Triple Goddess, many Wiccans worship different aspects of Cernunnos at different times.

First, we have his traditional horned form that's depicted as a human man with the horns of a stag. This is one of the oldest ways that humans have conceptualized him.

But it's not the only one!

In Celtic Wicca, you may also hear about the Green Man. While some witches conceptualize him as separate from the Horned God, I and many others see him as yet another facet within Cernunnos.

As the Green Man, Cernunnos is depicted as humanoid, but with leaves, branches, and vines covering his body. While the Horned God can be thought to represent animal life and animal nature, the Green Man is more of an expression of plant life in the natural world.

However, you might also see Cernunnos depicted as the Sun God—which one again reemphasizes his connection to nature. We'll take a closer look at the Sun God in the next section when we look at how Cernunnos relates to Wiccan holidays.

Finally, Cernunnos is also frequently depicted as the God of Death in Celtic Wicca. He is not a fearsome god in this role, though—he acts as a guide showing us the way from one life to the next.

Cernunnos and Wiccan Holidays

The eight Wiccan holidays, collectively referred to as the Wheel of the Year, celebrate the cycle of birth, life, death, and rebirth—and Cernunnos is at the center of that celebration.

Yule is the midwinter holiday that begins it all—this is the point of birth (or rebirth) for Cernunnos. Although the world is still cold and dormant at this point, his powers only grow from this point forward.

As the winter turns to spring, the relationship between Cernunnos and the Triple Goddess Brigid is emphasized. It is through their power that the beauty of nature is reborn.

Finally, we reach the summer solstice—the Wiccan holiday where Cernunnos (as the sun god) is at the height of his powers. Nature is in full bloom, and with his help, a good harvest isn't too far off.

As the autumn returns, the powers of the Horned God begin to weaken until we reach Samhain on October 31st—the holiday where we symbolically commemorate death and the fall of the Horned God.

But he's only gone for a short time! As always, Yule faithfully returns in the winter and with it, the new rise of Cernunnos to reenact the cosmic drama all over again!

Cernunnos and Christianity

Unfortunately, Cernunnos has been misconstrued by those who wished to lessen his influence among his followers. Medieval Christians frequently linked him with evil and the antichrist as they attempted to eradicate Paganism among the Celts.

And this, I'm sad to say, is why the modern-day Christian devil is often depicted with horns and cloven feet—he is a cruel and cartoonish parody of the much older (and kinder) Cernunnos.

The Horned God of Wicca is not someone to be feared, and he most certainly is not going to corral you into the flames of hell with a pitchfork! For Wiccans, Cernunnos is a father figure, not a villain.

People are free to mischaracterize the Horned God in any way they wish, but that doesn't make what they say true or useful. And I think the best way to counter these "arguments" is not to fight, but rather, worship Cernunnos without fear or apology.

Cernunnos Invocation to Honor the Dead

Because Cernunnos has so many associations with the cycle of life, death, and the underworld, he is the best Celtic god to turn to for rituals meant to honor the dead.

The following invocation is intended to bring comfort and peace when you lose a loved one. You'll be asking Cernunnos to ease your pain and provide safe passage to the next world for those who have moved on from ours.

This ritual can be performed any time you need it, but it's particularly suited for Samhain celebrations. And keep in mind that this can be performed for anyone—the recently deceased or someone who's been gone longer but you still want to honor.

Items Needed
- 1 black candle (or white candle with a black ribbon tied around it)
- Incense (cedar preferred but use what you have available)
- Matches or a lighter
- 1 memento of the person who has passed on (this could be a picture, an object of theirs, etc.)

Before you begin the ritual, be sure to clear a space for performing it. You'll need enough to walk a large circle on the floor.

To start, stand at the southernmost point of your space. Light the incense, hold it above your head, and say this:

I look into the underworld and call the great Cernunnos.

Now, begin walking a clockwise circle around your space. As you walk, hold the incense in your right hand and use your left to waft the smoke as much as possible.

Once you have returned to the southernmost point, repeat this:

Hail to the Horned God, keeper of the souls. I have prepared this sanctuary in your honor. I summon your power into this sacred space.

Place your incense down and move to the center of your circle. You should repeat the above invocation.

Finally, move to the northernmost point of the circle and say the invocation once more.

Return to the center of the circle and sit or stand for a moment with your eyes closed. Allow yourself to align with the energy of Cernunnos.

When you're ready to continue, collect your candle and your memento.

At the center of your space, light the candle and say this:

Great Cernunnos, guardian of the dead, I pray for the soul of [insert the person's name here]. Please ease my loss and provide them safe travel to the world beyond worlds.

Now, pick up the memento and hold it at a safe distance over the flame. The goal is to imbue this object with the sacred energy of the candle. As you hold it, visualize brilliant, white light surrounding the memento—then allow the energy to come to rest within the object itself.

When you're ready to continue, say the following:

I seal this object with the love of the Great Father of the forest. As I link myself to him, so do I link myself to the spirit of the departed. When this object is nearby, so too is the memory of their life. So mote it be.

To conclude the ritual, you will need to thank and dismiss Cernunnos. To do so, say this:

Hail and thanks to the mighty Horned God, protector of all. Let us depart from this place in love and peace. Blessed be until we meet again!

Immediately after saying the above, you should extinguish the candle to officially end the invocation.

The memento you blessed during the ritual should be kept in a special place where it won't be disturbed or harmed. When you feel yourself missing that special person, bring it out and remember that the watchful eye of Cernunnos is keeping them safe wherever they are.

CHAPTER 4: DAGDA, THE KING OF THE GODS

When it comes to deities of Ireland, not many are more important than the Dagda (sometimes referred to simply as "Dagda").

This powerful being, often depicted as a giant, bearded man in a cloak, was traditionally worshipped for his influence over many aspects of life—including time, the seasons, fertility, and magick.

Some Wiccans conceptualize Dagda as one aspect of Cernunnos the Horned God because of his status as fatherly figure and key Celtic deity. However, for our purposes, I'll be discussing him as distinct from the Horned God. I believe there are enough differences between the two to warrant this.

King of the Gods

In traditional Irish religion, Dagda is the king of the *Tuatha De Danann*—the people of the Goddess Danu. These mythological figures represent the earliest Irish gods and goddesses, and of them, Dagda stands alone.

The Tuatha possessed four legendary, magickal items—a stone, a sword, a spear, and a cauldron. And of these four, the cauldron is associated with Dagda. According to legend, any man who drank from his bottomless cauldron would never leave thirsty. And like Dagda, the cauldron was huge—the ladle was big enough to fit two people!

Father of the Triple Goddess

Like many of the traditional Celtic deities, Dagda's love life was...complicated. He fathered many other gods and goddesses by any number of different women.

However, for the purposes of Wicca, we're most interested in one of his daughters in particular—Brigid, the Triple Goddess. We've already discussed her origin story in this book, but it's worth mentioning this link between the two again.

Even though the Dagda may not be one of the principal deities of modern-day Celtic Wicca, his link to the Triple Goddess still affords him a place of importance. Additionally, his similarities to the Horned God (like his link to nature, protection, death, etc.) mean he is that much closer to the heart and soul of Celtic Wicca.

Dagda Correspondences

Because of his importance in traditional Irish myths, the Dagda has numerous magickal influences. This is by no means an exhaustive list, but these are the correspondences that I find to be the most important and powerful in my own magickal practice.

First and foremost, the Dagda is essential for spells of protection. The combination of his fatherly status and physically large stature give him the upper hand when it comes to the safety of his followers. Whether you're looking for physical, spiritual, or emotional safety, Dagda can help.

I think it's also important to emphasize his qualities as a source of magickal power for witches. In addition to possessing the legendary cauldron of the Tuatha De Danann, the Dagda was also keeper of a magickal staff, club, and harp. These are all highly symbolic of the spiritual energy that Dagda is capable of generating.

Finally, Dagda is very much connected with nature and the natural world—it's said that when he played his harp, the four seasons magickally arranged themselves in the correct order. While Cernunnos is also a god associated with nature, he corresponds more with animal life. Dagda, on the other hand, is a better choice for plant life.

Dagda Home Protection Invocation

Your home should be your safe space—it's the one place where you can temporarily unwind and disengage from the cares of the world.

In this invocation, we'll be calling upon Dagda to ask for his protection over your home, so that it truly can be the safe space you imagined.

Items Needed
- 1 medium-sized bowl
- Rosemary sprigs
- Rose petals
- Clover
- Basil leaves
- Pine needles or pine cones

(Item note: in this ritual, we'll essentially be creating a potpourri bowl, so there isn't an exact quantity for each of these plants. The bowl should simply be full when all is said and done.)

If logistics permit, this ritual should be performed in the entryway of your home. Since it acts as the "portal" to the outside world, it's a good place to have this rite of protection. However, if that's not a possibility, any room inside your home will do.

Begin in the center of your space with your hands apart and your eyes closed. Raise your hands above your head and repeat this invocation:

Great Dagda, king of the gods, I request your ear. Join me in this place that we may create magick.

Now, move to the northernmost point of your space and say this:

Hail from the north. Hail king of the gods!

Next, move to the south and repeat the line (switching out "north" for "south").

Repeat this process two more times at both the west and the east points of your space.

Once this is complete, return to the center of your space with eyes closed and hands above your head. Now say this:

The invocation is complete, and the Protector is near! Hail from your servant. Hail king of the gods! I call upon your power this day to protect my home and keep safe all within.

Now, take the rosemary and place it in the bowl. As you do, say this:

Rosemary, to keep our spirits pure.

Next, add the rose petals and say:

Rose, to extinguish hatred.

Up next is the clover:

Clover, to banish bad luck.

Then the basil:

Basil, to drive away bodily harm.

And finally, the pine needles or pine cones:

_____

Pine, the strong arms of the Protector.

_____

Take your completed bowl and stand in the north, then repeat the following blessing:

_____

May theses blessings of the Dagda keep my home secure. No spirit or man may harm those who enter. So mote it be.

_____

Place the bowl down at the northernmost point of your ritual space and return to the center to bid farewell to the Dagda. To do so, say the following:

Good tidings to the king of the gods as he departs in peace. Though I leave this place, I know your power still watches over me. Hail, thanks, and blessed be!

Once this ritual is complete, your bowl of plants is herbs is ready to be put to work! Over the next few days, I suggest leaving it in each room of your home for at least 24 hours apiece. After that, I suggest moving it to the entryway or another area of the home that is heavily trafficked.

This is a good ritual to repeat yearly to ensure protection for years to come!

CHAPTER 5: NICNEVEN, GIVER OF POWER

Within the Scottish pantheon, Nicneven is one busy Goddess! She is primarily the queen of the Fairies in traditional folklore, but she also rules over "strange creatures", nymphs and Spirits. In addition to these duties, she's also considered a patron Goddess of Witchcraft, which means she's got plenty of practitioners to worry about.

And on top of all that, she still finds time to be a Goddess of the Underworld and necromancy as well! In fact, you'll find that there are strong parallels between Nicneven in the Scottish tradition and Hecate in the Greek tradition.

Despite her many different associations, one thing is crystal clear about Nicneven— she is a Goddess that can bestow great power upon a witch. From the ability to communicate with Spirits to the ability to instantly recognize magickal plants, the magickal skill that this dark Goddess can grant a person is staggering.

However, don't just expect her to toss you a new ability like it's a piece of candy! Like most divine beings, petitioning Nicneven requires a gift to grease the wheels of the Spirit world. But you've also got to remember that she is a very maternal Goddess—if you're asking for something that Nicneven doesn't believe would be good for you to have, you can expect to leave empty handed.

Although Nicneven herself will never purposely deceive you, don't forget that she is the queen of Fairies. She may be trustworthy, but her followers are still prone to good-natured mischief, which can make working with her a bit of a headache if they are close by.

Nicneven Correspondences

Always show up with a gift when attempting to contact Nicneven. Like every good Scot, this Goddess is a fan of whiskey—and don't even think about skimping and buying something cheap! If whiskey isn't your thing, beer, cider, or mulled wine work too. If you're feeling particularly crafty, Nicneven will definitely appreciate it if your offering is homemade.

Otherwise, opt for something store bought but nice.

Fairies obviously spend a good amount of time in nature, so there are lots of plant and herbal associations with Nicneven. Some of the most common include bog myrtle, ivy, wildflowers, Scotch thistle, rowan, hazel, willow, and juniper.

Colors that work well with Nicneven include hunter green, off white, royal purple, and light gray.

Nicneven Invocation for Magickal Powers

This ritual is unlike any other in the book. Its guidelines are a bit more strict and unforgiving, but it is by far one of the most rewarding you will find, and it's a personal favorite of mine.

For this ritual, you'll need to take a little field trip into the great outdoors. In fact, you need to find a place that you can return to for up to nine nights in a row.

The location must be some sort of crossroads or a place where one thing begins and another ends. An actual crossroads is your best bet, but someplace like the edge of a lake or the edge of a forest can work as well. As long as it is a place of transition, Nicneven should appear.

Now, before you head out, you need to think long and hard about what kind of power you're going to ask Nicneven for. Don't fly through this process—be very thoughtful about your choice. Remember, the Goddess can always refuse your petition, but that's less likely if you've really given it some thought.

Most importantly, don't forget to bring a gift with you! Like I mentioned earlier, whiskey is a personal favorite of Nicneven. If you don't want to bring that, it should at least be some sort of alcoholic beverage—and don't skimp on quality. You don't need to bring an entire bottle with you every night. A bowl with a small amount poured in will do.

If Nicneven does not appear to you on the first night, you'll need to return again. Keep doing this until she finally appears or until you reach the ninth night—if you're not successful after nine tries, Nicneven is not going to grant you that specific power.

This is the process you should follow each time.

Begin by casting a sacred circle. Stand in the middle, lift your hands over your head, and say the following:

Goddess of the crossroads, I'm here to speak with you. Your power is undisputed in all the land. Who else can bestow the gift of magick upon humankind?

Now, pick up your offering bowl and raise it up over your head. Continue with the following:

I have not journeyed empty handed, great Nicneven, queen of the Fairies. May my gift warm your soul and grant me favor. If this is a fair trade, make yourself known.

Now, place the bowl back down on the ground. At this point, all you can do is wait. If Nicneven wants to show herself, she will. This can be in the form of a strong, sudden wind or she might even physically manifest in the form of an animal—typically a deer or a crow. If this happens, continue the ritual with the following:

Blessed be your presence to my eyes! My delight is all for you, mother Nicneven. If it pleases you, grant me the power to [insert your specific wish here].

Once you have made your petition known, there is no need to dally. Give Nicneven a short, personal thank you, and then close your sacred circle and get out of there! Nicneven is not a chatty Goddess—allow her to enjoy your offering in peace before she changes her mind.

If Nicneven does not make an appearance after you offer up your gift, don't continue with your petition. Close your sacred circle, pour the drink out on the ground, and try again the next night. The Goddess will typically make herself known within 20 minutes, so don't leave too early.

Remember, if Nicneven does not show up after nine nights, this is not a power that she wants to bestow on you. Additionally, if you're always petitioning her for new powers, she may grow tired of you and refuse to appear!

CHAPTER 6: RHIANNON, GODDESS OF THE MOON

Rhiannon is a mysterious figure from the Welsh tradition, which falls under the broader description of Celtic mythology. Her primary myths come from a medieval set of stories known as the *Mabinogion*.

Within these tales, Rhiannon is portrayed as a beautiful woman riding a white horse—and a powerful white witch to boot! Most importantly, she's regarded as the queen of the fairies, which makes sense, considering her name literally means, "Divine Queen."

In modern-day Wicca, these depictions of Rhiannon as a goddess of horses, fairies, and magick still hold. But, as you'll see in the next section, there is one unique association of hers which stands above the rest: the moon.

Goddess of the Moon

If you're familiar at all with Wicca, you already know that the moon plays an important role in our worship and practice. The Triple Goddess represents the changing phases of the moon, and the ritual of Drawing Down the Moon is one of the most sacred in our religion.

While Brigid may most commonly be associated with the moon because of her triple nature, Rhiannon is another important Celtic figure that we use to represent our celestial mother.

Unlike Brigid, however, Rhiannon's association with the moon are significantly "darker." These are not necessarily bad things, but she does more than just represent the moon—she also is a symbol of the nighttime itself, which also gives her associations with death.

That being said, Rhiannon is not a goddess to fear! She is very much a maternal figure to her followers—she doesn't bring death. Rather, she helps guide us through the murky depths of the world beyond ours. Throughout her sagas in the Mabinogion, she is depicted as full of love—she has nothing but kindness and wisdom to give.

Rhiannon Correspondences

Like I mentioned earlier, Rhiannon's primary correspondences include horses, magick, and the moon. But her attributes run even deeper than that, too.

Rhiannon is a good goddess to work with when it comes to animals, not only because of her horse, but also because of the three mysterious birds that are said to follow her. Images of either one of these animals will help you to establish a connection with her.

Additionally, this goddess also fits well into magick about music or poetry—which is probably why Stevie Nicks chose her as the subject for her song "Rhiannon."

Finally, Rhiannon is the goddess to call upon when trying to communicate with ghosts or spirits. Just as she helps guide us from this life to the next, she has the ability to help bridge the gap between our two worlds, if only for a moment.

Rhiannon Invocation for a Fresh Start

According to legend, Rhiannon was born at the moment the moon rose over the earth for the first time. In this invocation, we'll be linking her birth and ascension with the idea of starting anew. Just as Rhiannon experienced the newness of the moon, you too can know its rejuvenating power.

Whatever sort of fresh start you're looking for, it will be compatible with this ritual.

Items Needed
- 1 silver candle
- Matches or a lighter
- 1 quartz crystal (small enough to fit in your hands)

Ideally, this invocation should be performed on a new moon.

To begin, clear your ritual space and sit in the center. With your eyes closed and your hands above your head, repeat this:

In the silence, Rhiannon approaches.

Now, pick up your quartz—which is an offering to the goddess. As you do, say:

Great goddess of the moon, I request your presence here with me. May my offering be acceptable to the Divine Queen.

Next, carefully light your silver candle and place it in front of you. Gaze gently into the flame as you say this:

The flames of my past must be extinguished, I require their light no more. Rhiannon, gently guide me through to new life.

At this point, you should extinguish the candle. This represents your break from the past and beginning of your fresh start.

Take a moment to meditate and visualize the new beginning you're looking for. When you're ready, re-light the candle and continue:

The old has been made new. Life begins again. Mother moon, watch over me as I [here is where you should describe your fresh start]. May your divine presence always be near and give me the strength to continue the journey.

Now, stand up, pick up your candle and walk a clockwise circle around your space three times. For each rotation, you should say:

I am made new as Rhiannon ascends.

To finish the ritual, return the center of your space and repeat:

Though the flame may vanish, the light of Rhiannon is now within me.

You should quickly extinguish your candle after this.

Finally, you need to thank and say farewell to Rhiannon. To do so, say:

Mighty queen, moon goddess, white witch—you have made your presence known here with me. As we leave this space, I give you thanks and honor. I know you will guide me through this life and into the next. So mote it be.

After your ritual has ended, you should keep your quartz handy. If you don't want to carry it with you, leave it in a prominent place in your home as a reminder of your fresh start and the power of Rhiannon.

CHAPTER 7: MORRIGAN, GODDESS OF WAR

Morrigan is a fearsome Celtic deity, to say the least. She's most commonly known as a goddess of war with the ability to predict the outcome of battles. But despite what you might think, she's an important Celtic goddess to know and worship!

War, Fate—What's There to Like About Morrigan?

We have so many gentle, maternal goddesses within Wicca that it can be jarring to encounter one like Morrigan. Bloodshed and violence don't seem like areas that witches should be involved in.

Case in point—in one of her legends she is about to go to battle for the Tuatha De Danann against the Fomorians. When the leader of the Tuatha, Lugh, asks her what she expects to bring to the table, she replies that she intends to purse, subdue, and destroy the enemy.

And she keeps to her word, too!

When she enters the battlefield, she recites a poem that has the power to cast her enemies into the ocean. And after the victory is won, she recites another poem that predicts, not just the downfall of the Fomorians, but the world itself.

It's not exactly a great bedtime story.

But I would argue that Morrigan is more complex and nuanced than her affinity for violence. She also represents bravery and cunning on and off the battlefield. And because of her fierce nature, she makes a strong protector for her followers.

It would be wrong to downplay her associations as a war goddess, but it's also important to remember that, like humans, gods and goddesses can be confusing and complex creatures themselves.

Morrigan Correspondences

In several myths associated with Morrigan, she has the ability to transform into a crow. Because of this, crow imagery can help connect you to her power.

With her connections to war, colors like red and black often work well in rituals involving her. As does white, since it sometimes represents death.

In terms of Wiccan tools, Morrigan corresponds with the athame—or ceremonial dagger. Morrigan is a source of incredible spiritual power, and the athame can help to raise and direct that power.

Finally, herbs and plants like mugwort, myrrh, and mandrake all are good choices when invoking Morrigan.

Morrigan Invocation for Bravery

Even if you don't have any plans to head to the battlefield, we all have moments in our lives when we have to face scary situations and be brave. This invocation is meant to petition Morrigan for the power to make it through these situations.

A word of warning before we begin: Morrigan is not a mean deity, but she knows a weak and unsure witch when she sees one and is unlikely to lend her help to them. This ritual needs to be performed with the bravery and confidence you're looking for in the real world.

Items Needed
- 1 black feather
- Athame
- 2 red candles

To begin the ritual, clear your space and move to the northernmost point with your black feather. Once you're there, say this:

Great Morrigan, fly quickly from the north.

Now move to the south and say the same thing, but replace "north" with "south." You should do the same thing at the east and westernmost points of your space as well.

Next, return to the center and light your two red candles. As you do, repeat this:

The flames of war are lit. Morrigan draws near. Fearsome goddess, I bow before your mighty power.

At this point you should give a ceremonial bow to Morrigan.

Next, we move into the petition portion of the ritual. To begin this, say the following:

Phantom Queen, your bravery in battle knows no end. You hold the fates of men in your hand. As I move through this life, grant me the power to stand strong myself. I come before you fearless, seeking to stand fearless before the entire world. [If you have a specific situation that requires bravery, add it here.]

Now, raise hold the athame and raise it above your head with the point facing towards the ceiling. You should then say:

Winged goddess of the night, I call your power into the athame. With it, I shear cowardice from bravery, weakness from strength. All that remains is your might.

At this point, you should trace an equal-armed cross with the athame. Begin by moving top to bottom, and then trace left to right. Once this is done, hold the athame in your hands for a moment while you visualize the power running through it.

To end the ritual, say this:

Morrigan—you are protector, warrior, and queen. I feel your power within me. With your aid, I can face all that comes to me. I stand tall in your bravery and honor your legacy. I thank you for your favor as we depart this sacred place. So mote it be.

CHAPTER 8: AENGUS, GOD OF LOVE AND YOUTH

Within the Irish pantheon, Aengus is an important god of love and youth. If ever there were a deity to make you swoon, it's him! He's typically depicted as a young, beautiful man with birds circling his head—and we'll learn more about them in just a little bit. If all of that mushy stuff isn't your cup of tea, you'll be happy to know he's about more than just romance. Creativity, inspiration, and poetry also fall under his purview.

The Celtic Cupid

While there is no direct connection between Aengus and the Greek god Cupid, the similarities are definitely there. They're both young, beautiful, and associated with love. However, instead of magickal arrows to bring together lovers, Aengus uses his golden harp to weave a musical net, binding them together.

But his associations with love and romance don't stop there. According to some legends, Aengus transforms his kisses into the birds that fly around his head. He then uses these birds to send messages to those who seek his help in the ways of love.

Some people also say that when we sign off a letter with XOXO (hugs and kisses), the X's represent Aengus's birds and kisses. While it's true that the X's are indeed kisses, this practice seems to have originated with medieval Christians and not the ancient Celts.

Aengus Correspondences

A lot of the correspondences we associate with love also apply directly to Aengus. Colors like pink or red work well with him, as does bird imagery (songbirds and swans in particular), and plants like roses or lavender.

Because of his youth, rituals honoring or involving Aengus are at their most powerful during the early spring months—although it is acceptable to invoke him at any time of the year. If you're looking for very specific dates that work well with Aengus, I would suggest incorporating him into the celebration of the spring equinox (which varies yearly but usually falls sometime in late March) and Imbolg (which falls on February 1st). Imbolg is an early spring Wiccan festival, which fits in with Aengus, but please keep in mind that traditionally this holiday is associated with the goddess Brigid.

However, Aengus is also a god to remember at Samhain (October 31st). According to the myths, Aengus was having dreams about a beautiful woman that were so powerful he fell in love without even knowing who she was. Turns out, this woman was the goddess Caer who was being held captive with other women. Every other Samhain these women would be transformed into swans, and Aengus learned that if he could identify which swan was Caer, he would be allowed to marry her. Instead, Aengus turned himself into a swan and the two flew off together making beautiful music.

Aengus Invocation for Guidance in a New Relationship

New love is a wonderful and terrible thing. The highs are incredibly high and the lows are painfully low. When we're smitten, it seems that our capacity for being reasonable, thoughtful people is disabled in favor of pure, irrational bliss.

When embarking on a new relationship, you may have doubts—do I truly love this person or am I blinded by the joy of romance? It can be hard to navigate your feelings when they're so powerful and tumultuous.

In this invocation, I'll be showing you how to petition Aengus for guidance as you try to navigate the waters of love. His wisdom may be able to help you gain some insight into whether or not you've found "the one."

Items Needed
- 1 red candle
- 1 white candle
- Matches or a lighter
- Symbol of a bird (this can be a drawing, a picture, a feather, etc.)
- Silver ribbon (long enough to wrap and tie around both candles)

To begin, stand in the middle of your space and repeat this:

Aengus, god of love and youth, I call out for the wisdom of your song. You are unmatched in the truth of romance, and I seek to learn from you.

Arrange your candles so that the white one is on the left and the red one is on the right. The white candle represents wisdom and the red candle represents love. Now, wrap the silver ribbon (which represents Aengus) around the candles and tie a knot.

Light both candles (the white one first) while you say this:

Wisdom and love are united by your bond, fair Aengus.

Now, you should attempt to position your symbol of a bird behind the candles. The goal is to place it so that you have a comfortable line of sight that includes the two candle flames with the symbol between them.

Once that is in position, you can continue the ritual by saying the following:

As you sought Caer, I too seek my love. Great Aengus, I ask for guidance in my current relationship. Is this the path I should follow? Am I moving towards love? I humbly ask for any answers you wish to give.

Now, begin a comfortable gaze of the candle flames and the bird symbol in between them. Allow your mind to relax and open itself to the wisdom of Aengus. Remain in this state for as long as feels appropriate. Don't despair if you don't feel or see anything immediately—the purpose of this step is simply to create a link between you and Aengus. The messages will come in time.

Once you feel that you have gazed long enough, it's time to finish the ritual. To do so, say this farewell to Aengus:

Wise Aengus, keeper of the mysteries of love, you have made yourself known to me this day. Though the candles be extinguished and we leave this space, I await the messages you will bring to me in the future. So mote it be.

You should extinguish both candles immediately after saying this.

Once the ritual is done, you'll need patience as you wait for wisdom from Aengus. Sometimes this comes in the form of dreams, sometimes it's just a random thought that seems to pop into your head for no good reason. It's important to be on the lookout for these messages from him in the days and weeks that follow the ritual.

If you've performed the invocation but don't feel like you've heard back from Aengus, wait at least a month and try the ritual again.

By Didi Clarke

CHAPTER 9: DANU, MOTHER OF THE GODS

U nlike some of these other Celtic deities, not much information about Danu has survived into the modern day. What we do know is that she was considered the mother of the Tuatha De Danann, as that name literally means "children of the goddess Danu."

Who is This Mysterious Goddess?

Although many of Danu's myths have been lost to time, that doesn't mean we know nothing about her.

Because of her status as mother of the Tuatha De Danann, she can be viewed as a primordial creator goddess. This is exemplified by her associations with water—in ancient times, many cultures believed that before the world was created there was only this chaotic, primordial sea.

However, as a creator goddess, she is also closely tied to the earth and nature, as many other Celtic deities are as well.

Within the Wiccan context of the Triple Goddess, Danu obviously occupies the position of Mother. She is a gentle protector and source of comfort for her devotees. Unlike more fearsome deities, Danu is kind and approachable. She should be respected but certainly not feared.

Danu Correspondences

Of the four traditional elements, water and earth are the two most closely associated with Danu. Using them in combination with one another during a Danu ritual will provide even more power than using just one or the other.

Because of her associations with water, symbols of fish or other sea life work well. This is also probably why Danu has become associated with sailors and others who travel the seas.

Blue, green, brown, silver, and white are all colors that closely correspond with Danu. The blue represents water, while green and brown represent the earth, and silver and white are both associated with her divinity.

While circles are an important symbol in many aspects of Wicca, they are particularly associated with Danu—they emphasize both her protective nature and the completeness of her creation.

Early mornings are a good time for rituals involving Danu. It represents the birth of a new day similar to the birth she gave to the Tuatha.

Paradoxically though, the evenings are also a good time for Danu rituals, since she is associated with the Mother aspect of the Triple Goddess—a deity closely aligned with the moon.

Danu Invocation of Thanks

Most of the other rituals I've written for this book had some sort of purpose in mind—bravery, starting over, etc. For this final invocation, I wanted to do something different. Instead of petitioning Danu for something, it is simply an expression of worship to her. She is considered the mother of all, so I'd say she deserves it!

Like I mentioned in the correspondences section, this would be a perfect fit for early morning. It's a great way to start your day on a positive note. It could be performed in the evening, but in this specific instance, I would strongly suggest the morning.

Items Needed
- Small bowl of water
- Bright, colorful flower (any kind will do)
- Handheld bell
- 1 white or silver candle
- Matches or a lighter

To begin, walk a clockwise circle around your ritual space three times. As you walk, ring your bell loudly and repeat this:

Hail to the Queen of All! Hail to the Creator Goddess! Hail to the Mother of the Gods!

Now, move to the center of your space. Put your bell down and raise your hands above your head while you say:

Ancient Danu, who was before all being, I welcome you into this sacred space. May my words please you and my actions bring you honor. Let all of creation hear of my devotion to you.

Next, bring your bowl of water to the westernmost point of your circle. Raise it in the air as you say this:

Ancient Danu, keeper of the primordial sea, the power of water is yours. Both changeless and always changing, the river of your might flows forever.

You should leave the bowl of water at this western point. Then, move to the southernmost point of the circle with your flower. Raise it in the air and repeat:

Ancient Danu, keeper of the wise land, the power of earth is yours. Your care and protection is unmoving.

Once again, leave the flower at the southern point and move to the northernmost point with your candle. Light it and say:

Ancient Danu, keeper of the divine flame, the power of spirit is yours. Always near and everywhere, you keep watch over all that is.

Leave the candle there and move to the center of your circle one last time. Ring your bell three times and in a loud voice, say this:

Now and forever, hail to Danu, great mother of the Triple Goddess and the Horned God. Hail to Danu, mother of the Tuatha De Danann. Hail to Danu, mother of all. Hail, hail, hail!

Once the ritual is complete, you should extinguish your candle immediately. Although it should not be used for other, unrelated rituals, I encourage you to light it over the next few days and weeks until it is completely used. It will serve a continual reminder of the goddess Danu.

CHAPTER 10: KEEPING THE SPIRIT OF THE CELTS ALIVE

Much of the history of the ancient Celts and their practices have been lost to time. It's likely we'll never know the full story of how they practiced their religion. But the power of their myths and deities can still have an impact on us today.

Even though Celtic Wicca may not be a faithful reconstruction of this ancient, mysterious belief system it embodies the spirit of the stories passed down to us by the Celts. Wicca (and religion in general) can be a transformative experience for practitioners, but there are times when the practices themselves are transformed as well.

It's my hope that this book will allow you to be part of that transformative process. These deities may be ancient, but they still have to power to change our lives for the better, even in the modern age.

Blessed Be,

Didi

CHAPTER 11: READ MORE FROM DIDI CLARKE

The Wiccan Bible for the Solitary Witch

Are you a spiritual seeker who marches to the beat of your own drum? Are you looking to explore the world of Wicca while still maintaining your independent spirit?

The Wiccan Bible for the Solitary Witch is the ultimate resource for learning the fundamentals of witchcraft as a freethinking, solo practitioner!

Didi Clarke has been studying the art of Wicca for over a decade as a solitary witch, and in that time, she's published numerous books about all aspects of the craft. She has an intimate knowledge of the joys and pitfalls of studying Wicca without the aid of a coven. Now that expertise can be yours too!

In *The Wiccan Bible for the Solitary Witch*, you'll find easy-to-understand descriptions and explanations of the most important aspects of being a practicing Wiccan. Knowledge that was once a closely guarded secret of traditional covens can be yours to learn and apply to your own spiritual practice!

In particular, this book will teach you things like:
- Wiccan Ethics

- Important Wiccan Terms
- How Magick Works
- Wiccan Holidays
- How Wiccans Pray
- Writing Your Own Spells
- Performing Rituals
- And much more!

This information is a must-have if you're a solitary witch who wants to experience the liberating power of magick in your own life. It's a self-guided manual for anyone who values their unique perspective and wants to become a successful Wiccan!

Buy *The Wiccan Bible for the Solitary Witch* today!

The White Magick Spell Book

Unlock the Power of Light and Goodness in the World!

White magick is all about making the world a better place for yourself and all living creatures. Within the pages of *The White Magick Spell Book*, you'll find the rituals, spells, and information you need to make this better world a reality!

To some extent, we're all born with a natural desire to practice compassion towards other living things. But you'll find that as you delve deeper into this branch of witchcraft that your compassion will begin to grow even more, until being a help to others is second nature. White magick has many practical benefits, but I you'll find that the most important one is the transformation that takes place within your soul!

What You'll Find

Each of the spells you'll find in *The White Magick Spell Book* are broken down into easy, step-by-step instructions with plenty of explanatory notes to guide you through the process. It's important to understand the "why" of magick just as much as the "how."

However, it's my hope that these spells and rituals will help to expand the spiritual horizons of even the most experienced witch. They're all one-of-a-kind, original creations based on my own observations in the craft—you won't find these spells anywhere else!

When you read *The White Magick Spell Book*, you'll find a wide variety of magick meant to spread light and life. These include:

- Home Protection
- Emotional Healing
- Banishing Negativity
- Communicating with Guardian Angels
- Building Friendships
- And Much More!

The World of White Magick Awaits You!

Are you ready to experience all the benefits that white magick has to offer? Then buy *The White Magick Spell Book* today and witness its power for yourself!

The Wiccan Handbook of Candle Spells

Are you ready to tap into the magickal power of candles?

The Wiccan Handbook of Candle Spells is the ultimate resource for learning and practicing the art of candle magick!

Didi Clarke has been a Wiccan practitioner for over a decade, and in that time, she's published numerous books about all aspects of the craft. In The Wiccan Handbook of Candle Spells she shares her personal secrets for unlocking the spiritual power of the element of fire!

When you try these one-of-a-kind spells for yourself, you'll understand why candles are one of your most powerful tools as a witch. The Wiccan Handbook of Candle Spells is here to teach you things like:

- Candle blessings
- Banishing negativity
- Invoking deities
- Communication with the spirit world

- And much more!

In addition to original spells, this book is also a resource for understanding the philosophy behind candle magick. It's a one-stop guide to learning both the "how" and "why" of candle spells!

Whether you're new to the world of Wicca or are an experienced witch, *The Wiccan Handbook of Candle Spells* has something for you! These rituals pack serious power, but they're presented in an easy-to-understand, step-by-step format. Candle magick is an exciting, must-have tool for witches of all levels!

Buy *The Wiccan Handbook of Candle Spells* today!

Find me on Twitter at @AuthorDidi
And be sure to like my Facebok page: facebook.com/authordidiclarke
You can contact me via email at authordidiclarke@gmail.com

Printed in Great Britain
by Amazon